To the Rescue!™

Emergency Helicopters

Joanne Randolph

PowerKiDS press™
New York

For Riley, Deming, and Hannah

Published in 2008 by The Rosen Publishing Group, Inc.
29 East 21st Street, New York, NY 10010

Copyright © 2008 by The Rosen Publishing Group, Inc.

First Edition

Book Design: Greg Tucker
Photo Researcher: Nicole Pristash

Photo Credits: Cover, pp. 5, 7, 9, 11, 15, 17, 23, 24 (top left), 24 (top right), 24 (bottom left) Shutterstock.com; p. 13 © Justin Sullivan/Getty Images; pp. 19, 24 (bottom right) by Jay C. Pugh/U.S. Navy via Getty Images; p. 21 by NyxoLyno Cangemi/U.S. Coast Guard via Getty Images.

Library of Congress Cataloging-in-Publication Data

Randolph, Joanne.
    Emergency helicopters / Joanne Randolph. — 1st ed.
        p. cm. — (To the rescue!)
    Includes index.
    ISBN 978-1-4042-4151-0 (library binding)
    1. Helicopters in search and rescue operations—Juvenile literature. 2. Helicopter ambulances—Juvenile literature. I. Title.
    TL553.8.R36 2008
    629.133'352—dc22

                                        2007021211

Manufactured in the United States of America

Contents

Watch out for the **blades**! Here comes an emergency helicopter to save the day!

Helicopters have four blades.
These blades help helicopters
fly forward, up and down, or
float in one spot.

Helicopters can be used to bring sick or hurt people quickly to a **hospital**.

Helicopters can help save people from drowning.

Helicopters can help people who are trapped by floods.

Helicopters can help people who are trapped on the side of a **mountain**.

Helicopters can even help put out fires.

Rescuers can be lowered from the helicopter using a rope.

Some helicopters have a rope with a bed at the end. Sick or hurt people are lifted to safety in this bed.

We count on the people who work with emergency helicopters every day.

Words to Know

blades

hospital

mountain

rescuer

Index

Web Sites

Due to the changing nature of Internet links, PowerKids Press has developed an online list of Web sites related to the subject of this book. This site is updated regularly. Please use this link to access the list:
www.powerkidslinks.com/ttr/eheli/